Dedication

This book is for all the Grafham Girls...the patchworkers, beaders, spinners and and sewers...you have made my life so much fun! Thank you all for your encour laughter. You ROCK! xxx

Thank you to Mia Chipchase and Grace Richards for modelling these face masks, during lockdown 2020... I took the photos at a distance! I love the way your beautiful eyes smile above the masks.

I would also like to thank Hope Richards for her faces on page 6 and Gareth Neal for his dog face design modelled here by Grace.

Stay safe xxx

I started to write this book in 2018... after so many people asked me to do it and share my way of making faces. I have been procrastinating over it since then! I never dreamed that all our lives would change in the way they did in March 2020 when Covid 19 hit the UK and gripped us all in fear of catching the deadly virus. The world went into lockdown and for me, I was one of the lucky ones as I love to make and create and was able to throw myself into making masks for the local care home as well as make scrubs and scrubs bags to help the NHS.

I know many of you reading this will have done the same and it has been lovely being part of such a big, caring community. We taught our granddaughter Hope to drive during lockdown, as we went around the area collecting scrubs, scrub hats, ear angels, bags and fabrics and then delivering them to local hospitals, GP surgeries and dental clinics. All journeys had to be necessary and essential... so they qualified!

Mask wearing became very common and in some countries, it was a legal requirement to wear them in public. I was going to say it has not happened here yet, but probably would after the book was printed... but today, 4th June, as I was proof reading this, the instruction has gone out to say masks must be worn on public transport from 15th June. I had already decided to include face mask designs and instructions, as I think they will be here to stay a while. We all love to see smiling faces as we are not used to having our own expressions hidden, so I have created some faces for you to copy or be inspired by; to create your own.

I have been wearing a mask in public since the start and have enjoyed making my mask a bit of fun. At first, I free machined the words...'if you can read this you are too close!' across the top... I wanted the mask to remind people to keep well back! Now, I simply want to have a selection of looks to choose from... as well as colours to match different outfits!

I have worked out a quick way of making masks and of getting the elastic length right for different people... all of which I am sharing here. As we all know, two layer fabric masks are not surgical quality and simply help to prevent you from contaminating others... but the cumulative effect is multiplied if everyone wears one. They would work for reducing pollution too... I could have done with one in India!

As these designs are free machine stitched, it does mean there are holes in the fabric, so I suggest you might like to add an extra layer... but do audition the fabrics together to make sure you can breathe comfortably if you do!! You could draw them onto the fabric with indelible pen if you prefer not to stitch the fabric, making tiny holes.

Acknowledgements

A special thank you to Tony for putting up with me and my mess and helping me when I go out and give talks and play days when I can share the fun with so many people.

Suppliers

Dy-Na-Flow by Jacquard, procion dyes, pelmet Vilene and Bondaweb are available by mail order from Rainbow Silks in Amersham, along with other haberdashery supplies. Tel 01494 727003 Email caroline@rainbowsilks.co.uk

Introduction

I can't draw. I have never been able to draw and I know that because my art teacher told me I was no good. In the 1980's I had to start to draw as I had a machine knitting business called Tiny Tiger and I wanted to draw the designs so the knitters could make them. My designs were painfully simple but that naivety made them successful. Do you remember them?

That was a long time ago. Since then, slowly, I have learnt how to get my ideas down on paper and in recent years have finally overcome the hurdle of 'I can't draw' as I have been creating my machine stitched originals for my greetings card designs. Faces, however, were a different story. I made a small hanging called Cupcake Fairy and loved making it. I kept putting off the face till last. I really enjoyed stitching her hair in long, carefree strands of free machine stitch in black thread. When I came to sew her face in the space left, she looked as if she had been punched. Her features were wrinkled up as I should have stitched her face first while the fabric was flat! See Gallery page 46.

It was this quilt which made me think there had to be a better way and here it is. I liken it to washing the floor before cooking pancakes on Shrove Tuesday….this is to guarantee that they will not drop on the floor and if they do then the two second rule applies (unless my daughter's dog is around and beats me to it!) Equally, if you make the head separately you can ditch it if you don't like it or you can add a hat at a jaunty angle to hide an ugly part of her face but the chances are it will be fun and quirky and add life to your quilt. Go ahead and try it for yourself.

I hope that you enjoy creating your own characters using the techniques in this book to set you free to add some very interesting people to your work!

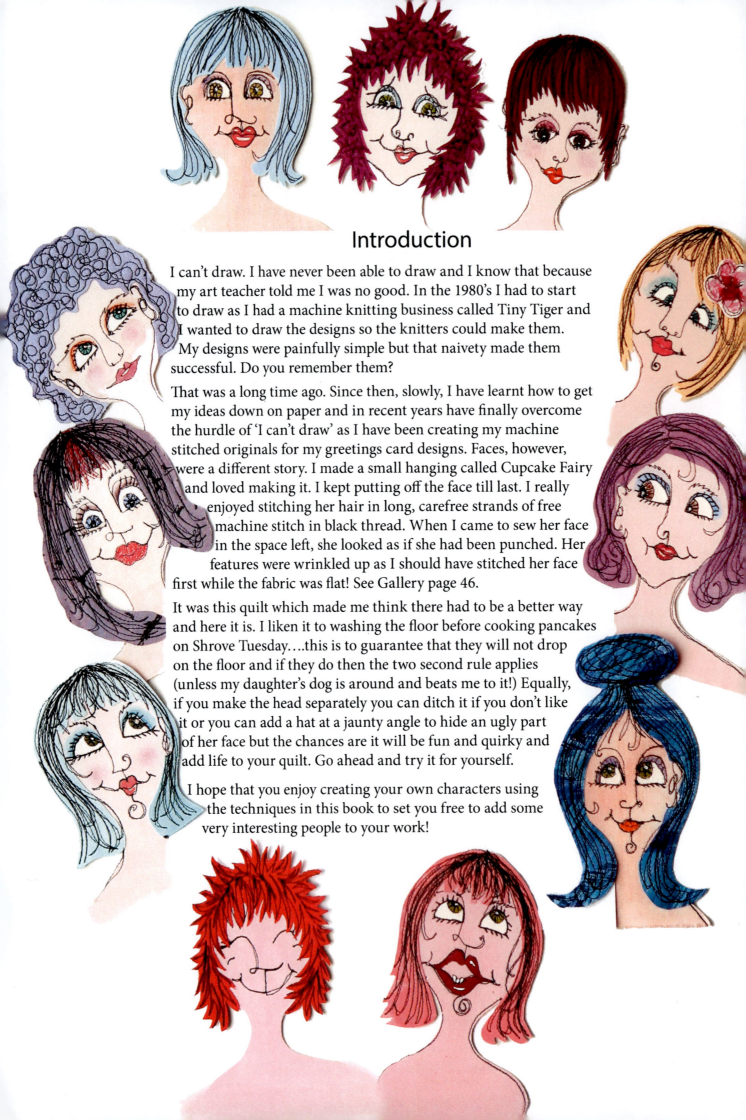

You will need...

Pelmet Vilene S80 10T

Bondaweb or other heat fusible web

Pencil or

Time fading, water fading or heat erasable pen

Iron and board

Silicone baking sheets x 2 for protection against the heat fusible glue!

Pink, tan or flesh coloured fabric

Procion dyes if you wish to dye your own or

Dye-na-flow in ecru, ochre and hot fuchsia to

paint fabric in a nice selection of flesh tones!

Acrylic or fabric paints, or Inktense for the features

Plastic sheeting to protect your worktop

A lovely selection of fabric scraps for the clothing, backgrounds, accessories and hair

Scissors for cutting fabric and tiny curved or double curved scissors which are handy for snipping threads close to the work

Black thread

You will also need...

A sewing machine with a darning or free motion foot.
You will also need to be able to lower or cover the feed dogs to free machine stitch

Beads and buttons, needle and hand sewing kit

Drawing Faces

These faces were drawn by my granddaughter Hope when she was ten years old... I just love the way she has stepped away from convention and given them funny eyes and mouths. Aren't they fun?

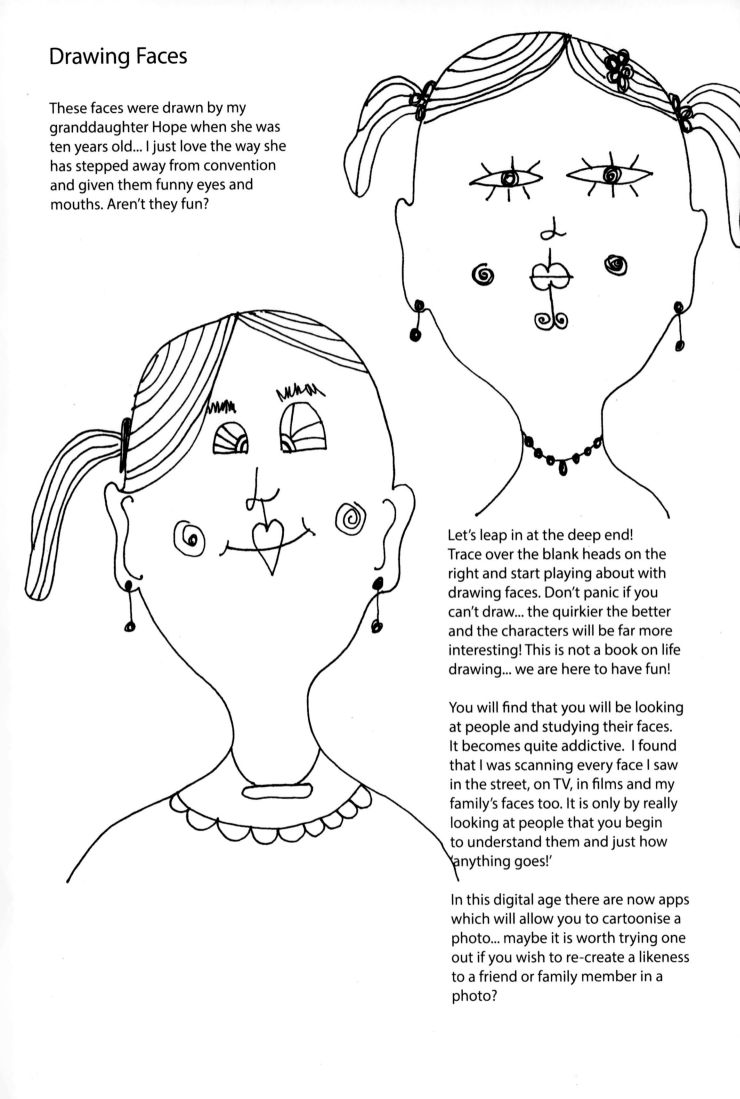

Let's leap in at the deep end! Trace over the blank heads on the right and start playing about with drawing faces. Don't panic if you can't draw... the quirkier the better and the characters will be far more interesting! This is not a book on life drawing... we are here to have fun!

You will find that you will be looking at people and studying their faces. It becomes quite addictive. I found that I was scanning every face I saw in the street, on TV, in films and my family's faces too. It is only by really looking at people that you begin to understand them and just how 'anything goes!'

In this digital age there are now apps which will allow you to cartoonise a photo... maybe it is worth trying one out if you wish to re-create a likeness to a friend or family member in a photo?

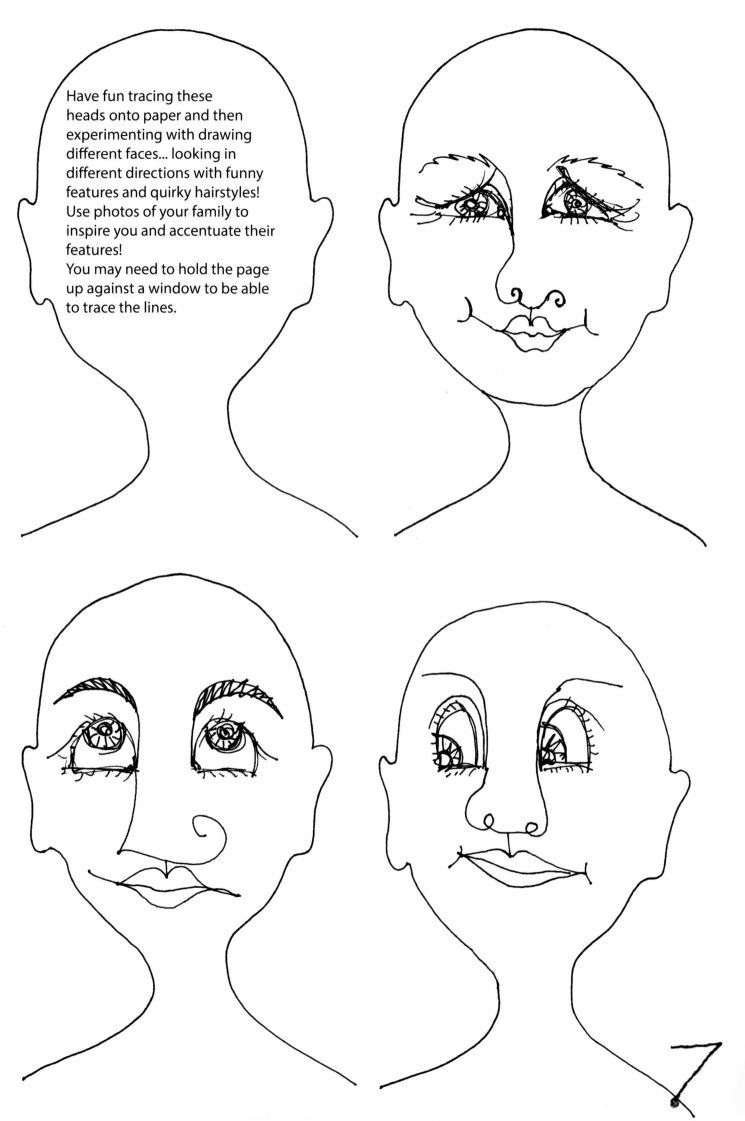

Make a start

Look closely at eyes. Had you noticed that inner line before? Look at yourself in the mirror. Take a selfie with your phone and then zoom in (if you dare!) and study the shapes of your own eyes. Now practice drawing lots of eyes.
Make some big and round, draw some almond shaped, make some flat across the bottom. Draw eyes close together, wide apart, high, low or in extreme proportions.

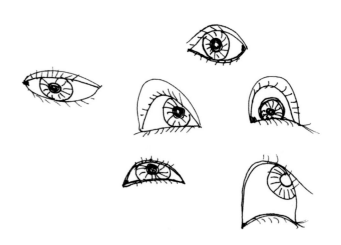

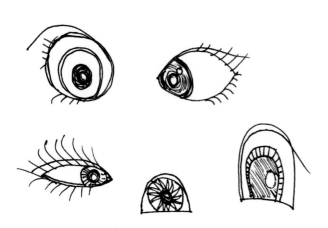

Practice drawing the pupils inside the eyes. Notice how the whole of the iris, the coloured circle, is not always on show. See how it gets cut off by the eyelids. Now take your time studying eyelids and you will see a huge variation in the length of lashes. Remember when you are making your own faces you can really accentuate the features and making long lashes makes the character more whimsical.

Eyebrows are fascinating and are very popular at the moment with a craze for stencilled OTT blades so feel free to try and replicate them with some funky heavy free machining or appliqué!

Next, move on to studying noses and the way people look at you. When someone 'looks down their nose' at you, draw the nose extra long and have the eyes higher so the head looks as if it is tilted back slightly in disdain.

Some noses are very wide, some pointed but all add character to the face.

Finally look at mouths. My favourite are the wide smiley friendly ones with full lips and turned up corners. Some people have dimples when they smile. When you are drawing faces, don't worry about how you are going to stitch them. We will worry about that later!

Keep on drawing and sketching and playing at creating your own characters. Try as many variations as you can and have them looking left or right, looking up or down or simply looking straight ahead. Once you are happy that you have drawn something you like you are ready to move on.

Linking up the feature lines

There are no rules to how you free machine sew your face. If you look carefully at my faces, you will see some have been machined continuously and some separately. It really does depend on the look you want and whether the features run into each other or not.

Sometimes I like to work one side of the face in one, starting from the outer edge of the eyebrow and then working down to the eye, then draw around the eye, then again adding the inner lid then I like to add the lashes before drawing in the iris and the pupil. I continue down the nose and then into the lips, working around them to give each part two lines. I have drawn an example for you so you can see how I build up the lines.

I am left handed ... (smiley face!) You may prefer to reverse my way of working and will probably rather sew the right side of the face in one go. Experiment! Finish drawing any remaining features of the face. You might find it helpful to repeat the drawing exercise before attempting to sew it.

Marking the features

There are two ways of marking the features that I have used. The first faces I made, I drew on the back of the heads with pencil. To do this, tape your drawing onto a window, turning it over first to reverse it. Next, put the fabric head over it with the fabric face down against the drawing. Use a pencil to draw the face onto the pelmet Vilene.

I must say I'd rather draw the face directly onto the faces and I enjoy using a heat erasable pen, or a water soluble or fading pen. Tape the face drawing on the window the right way round this time and place the fabric face over it with the fabric side facing. Use a very light touch to draw as little as possible.

With heat erasable pens there is always a 'ghost line' visible after using them once the line has disappeared when you iron it. A word of warning... if the fabric is kept in a very cold room the lines may re-appear so do not use on any precious work. We don't know what the long term effect of these pens will have on fabrics. I am now favouring the water soluble pens and rinse my work well under running water to remove the ink and then lay the face flat on a clean towel to dry.

Adding the extras…

If you want to add glasses to your character, machine the whole face first. This way the eyes will look more natural when you add the glasses over the top. You can use either organza or acetate for the lenses but do beware using your iron anywhere near the acetate and keep the temperature low for organza! I have given you full instructions on page 16 for a really quick and easy way to make them.

Earrings, necklaces, tattoos and piercings all add character and another great excuse to raid your stash to find something suitable to use. The tiny 'brads' used in card making and scrapbooking are perfect!

For the clothes, I have been trying to use up pieces of fabric I have dyed, painted and printed in my City and Guilds days... it is a really good excuse to use up your experimental pieces if you have any, as it adds uniqueness to you work.

Painting or dyeing the fabric?

For speed, painting fabric works well to create the flesh tones you are looking for and is immediate. It is a good idea to paint several batches, varying the colour mix, so that your characters are not all identical but make sure you label each batch of painted fabric in case you want to add arms at a later date!

You will need..

Fabric paints...I have used liquid Dye-na-flow but you can use any fabric or acrylic paints as long as you dilute them well.
Either a dropper, for measuring small quantities of or a set of measuring spoons if you have them. I found a set on the internet with the names a tad =1/4 tsp, dash =1/12 tsp, pinch =1.16 tsp, smidgen =1/32 tsp, and a drop.
Rubber gloves
Old cotton sheeting as it absorbs the paints evenly. If you are using new material, hot wash it once or twice to remove the dressing

Painting fabrics

This is a really quick and easy way of getting the perfect colour for your faces. Alternatively you can dye your own fabrics using procion dyes or take the easy way out and simply buy the colour you want!

Here, I am using just three colours...hot fuchsia, ochre and ecru. The easiest way to measure out the colour is to use a dropper or a set of tiny spoons. I suggest you make your own samples and then you can simply multiply the quantities to paint your cloth. Always remember to wet the cloth first and mix the colours thoroughly.
I do not use white to lighten the colour, I simply use more water to create pale shades. Measuring the water is essential too if you want to be able to reproduce colours.

There are plenty of permutations you can try...here are some ideas
2 drops of hot fuchsia pink alone
1 hot fuchsia pink plus 1 ochre
1 hot fuchsia pink plus 1 ecru
1 hot fuchsia pink plus 2 ochre
1 hot fuchsia pink plus 2 ecru
2 hot fuchsia pink plus 1 ecru
2 hot fuchsia pink plus 1 ochre

There are many more you can try depending on the look you want... more ochre will give more of a tanned look.

All the above can be lightened with more water. Once painted, leave the fabric on a flat surface to dry. You can use a hair dryer to speed up the drying process but I will advise you against laying it on a radiator to dry...the colour will become very uneven. Again, experiment to find what works best for you.

Tip
Measuring spoons are especially useful if you are dyeing fabrics.

Dyeing fabrics

Using paints is a quick and easy way of producing a nice selection of flesh coloured fabrics, but if you have procion dyes in the house... use them very sparingly. It is a good idea to let the dye soak into the fabric well before adding any soda ash to the mix as this will help the fabric to be an even shade.

There are plenty of tutorials online if you wish to have a go at fabric dyeing. Just be sure to make plenty of each batch of colour!
Make a note of fabric weight and dye measurements so you can repeat any successful colours.

Free Machining

Free motion sewing is great fun once you have mastered it but I want to give you a few hints and tips to help you, if you are new to it or find it a bit of a struggle.

I always practise on paper first, often without even putting any thread in the machine. Not all machines will sew without thread… some of the new ones are quite bossy about such things. No worries… you can use fabric and paper behind it, or vice versa, then thread up your machine as normal. Paper is stable enough to sew on without having to bother about layering up fabric with wadding and backing.

Before you begin, fit your free motion foot to the machine… making sure it is the correct one for your model of machine. This is really important. Drop or cover the feed dogs following the instructions in your machine manual. If you have a 'needle down' button, use it as the needle will stop in your work and hold it in place if you stop to move your hands.

If you have a favourite quilting aid like quilter's gloves, do use them. I always use two little pieces of rubber shelf matting cut to 2" x 3" which fit perfectly under the three fingers used for quilting. They give you super grip… the secret to quilting little details. Make sure your chair is high enough too… or cut the table legs down as I have on my little sewing table! Ideally, your arms should be at right angles as you work.

Let's practise… I have given you a page to copy for free machining. Trace or copy it onto paper if you like. It is a good loosening up exercise. Do this with no thread if you can. The secret when you are free machining is to keep sewing… keep your foot on the accelerator as you move your hands. It's a bit like patting your head and rubbing your tummy…practice makes perfect! Keep the paper upright as you sew using your hands to move it under the needle. Do not be tempted to turn the paper as you sew.

Make sure your rubber grippers are on the paper and not over the edge as this will prevent the paper moving freely.

Keep your hands fairly close to where you are sewing. If you need to move your hands closer…stop sewing… move your hands, then carry on sewing. Don't worry about following the lines exactly… simply use them as a guide.

When you are sewing the 'v' shapes, stop your hands momentarily at each point, allowing the needle to dance on the point… push… stop… pull… stop… push… stop… pull… stop. This way you will get perfect, sharp points. This method is the one you will use for drawing the eyes, lips eyebrows and noses. Just keep your foot on the pedal and keep a good speed going.

If you drive too slowly you will get big, angular stitches. You need little stitches when sewing eyes and eyebrows. Avoid setting your speed controller on slow… instead, try and use your foot to control the speed if you can.

When you are sewing eyelashes think to yourself… along stop… out stop… back stop… along stop. Practise on paper over and over and it will help you to gain confidence. Just PLAY! Drawing with pen on paper is a great way to get practise too.

You will probably need to lower your top tension slightly for free machining although some machines have automatic tension. Refer to your manual for help.

Once you have threaded up your machine, put the presser foot down and then take one stitch, lift the presser foot and bring up the thread from underneath. If your machine has a thread cutter there is no need for this step.

If you want to move from one area of the work to another, do not cut the threads. Simply lift the presser foot and needle, move the fabric, lower the foot and carry on sewing. You can cut off the threads after a few stitches to get them out of the way. I never sew in the ends. I always start and stop with a little flurry of stitches to make the work secure.

The picture you are making does not have to stand up to the rigours of washing. It is a different matter for a bed quilt!

Opposite, I have given you a practice page to help you loosen up for free machining and some of the lines and shapes you will be sewing when creating your own faces. You will notice that some of the lips are single lined, some double and some have curly smiles as the sides. Play around and see what you like. Try and give each of your characters his or her own features and have fun!

Free machining practice page...
Copy this onto paper and then have a go at sewing it with no thread

Creating the faces

I have made the faces fit comfortably onto A4 so you can trace them easily. It is a good size to start with.

Trace the head onto the paper side of Bondaweb. Roughly cut out the Bondaweb just outside the lines.

Turn it over and iron it onto the back of your 'face' fabric. Use the silicone sheets to protect your iron and board from any accidental bondage!

Cut the head shape out on the lines and then peel off the backing paper.

Place the fabric, glue side down onto the pelmet Vilene, cover and press in place.

Hold up to a window or light box and trace around the head on the back...IF you want to sew from the back. Omit this stage if you are sewing directly onto the front. You can then lightly draw the features as a sewing guide.

Set the sewing machine for free motion...see page 12... If sewing from the BACK, increase the upper thread tension slightly and use the same thread in the bobbin. If sewing from the front, reduce the tension.

There is no need to try and sew the face in one go... if you need to move to a different area, simply lift the needle and presser foot and carry on sewing. Clip or sew in the threads later.

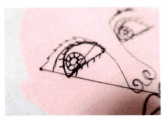

For her hair, I turn the piece over and hold it up to a window and trace the outline of the head then I can add the outlines of the hair which may or may not cover the eyes, or ears! Once you are happy, trace the hair shape onto Bondaweb and cut out and bond it in place as with the head.

Start to free machine her hair... take one stitch and pull the bobbin thread to the top before you begin. I like to start at the top of the head and sew fast and free to get long flowing strands of hair. If you are going to cut out the head, avoid sewing over the edge of the hair fabric!

I use acrylic paints to add the features, but fabric paint or Inktense will work well. Just practise on spare fabric first as the paint can bleed if too wet and look ugly if applied too thick!

To make her lips look glossy, use a light touch of white paint across them and give a highlight to both eyes too... in the same place!

At this point, she is still surrounded by the pelmet Vilene... add any hats or hairpieces if you like before cutting her out.

Finally...cut her out carefully avoiding snipping any of the stitching on her hair... then you are done!

Faces come in all different shapes and sizes and the size you make yours will depend on what you want to do with it. All the faces for my 'Sewing Machine Girls' are just 4" tall and about 10" high on 'Don't Forget to Drop the Dogs' on page 46.

Instructions for making the glasses are on page 16... and a great way of covering up eyes which did not go well... as well as creating great characters.

Adding glasses...fiddly to make, but worth it!

These big blue glasses are perfect for covering up a less that perfect face... or simply giving character! Turn the 'face' over and trace around the eyes using Bondaweb, for the frames, and roughly cut out. Iron onto the back of the black fabric and cut out on the lines.

Draw onto the back of your chosen lens fabric and cut out adding a little extra. Cut out the lenses. Peel the backing from the frames and then place the lenses onto a silicone sheet, right side up and lay the frames over them, right side up. Cover with silicone and press.

Once cool, you can peel the glasses off the silicone sheet and then position the glasses onto the face. When you are happy they are in the right place, cover again, lightly press, then free machine around them.

Here are the 'pince nez' glasses being worn by Edwina on page 21. I have used a textured, iridescent organza for the lenses and used the technique above. It is worth buying good, small sharp scissors for this!

How I love any excuse to go to the charity shop or a car boot sale! I have a jar filled with broken jewellery but I have found it so useful when I have wanted to add earrings and other accessories to my quilts.

These colourful wooden buttons given to me recently will be perfect as earrings… and can be sewed on using colourful stranded embroidery cotton.

The girl on one of my early quilts… 'Don't Forget to Drop the Dogs' on page 46 is wearing a pair of earrings I won in a Christmas cracker! The problem is it becomes impossible to throw anything out as it may come in useful one day!

Henrietta

Henrietta is wearing a dress made from hand dyed fabric which was hand printed with a stamp made from funky foam. The purple shapes were printed at random and then they were embellished with silver gutta... silk painting outliner. Her earring was made in the same way.

Her hair piece was made and the flower added, before the pelmet Vilene was cut away and then it was hand embellished with beads and sequins. To sew a sequin on easily... put the needle into the back of it and let it fall, cup side up onto the fabric. Thread up a tiny seed bead and then push it down onto the sequin before taking a stitch back through the sequin to the back of the work. Secure with a few stitches before moving on to the next sequin.

When painting her face, make sure you remember to add white highlights to her lips and eyes to make them look shiny.

Edwina

I really loved making this character with her long nose and neck and her fabulous, purple hair pulled up high on her head. She really does look as if she is looking down her nose at you and the addition of 'pince nez' seemed to suit her perfectly. See page 16 for instructions.
I like to make the glasses separately which means you can audition them on the face and then, once you are happy with the position, you can iron them in place before stitching them.

I drew this character on the front using a heat erasable pen... but do remember the danger of using these pens is that they leave a ghost line visible and the lines may return in very cold conditions! They are great for speed and to help you gain confidence but other methods are safer.

I used a very light touch with a dry sponge to give the cheeks a slight blush and golden shadow to her blue eyes.

My Mum used to be a very prolific lace maker and I love to use her lace when I can. This eyelet lace has been threaded up with some hand dyed purple fabric and then added to the neckline.

Her dress is made with delicious Kaffe Fasset fabric. I decided to position the 'pince nez' low on her nose...I will sew them in place when I am sure I know exactly where I want them!

Gardenia

Here you can see the difference the stitching makes to the hair. I always like to use black thread to really give it a punchy look but you may prefer to use the same colour or a darker shade.

For her face, I stitched it all in one go! I marked her features on the front of the fabric and then started on the outer edge of her eyebrow, into the eye and then down into the first side of her nose, her smiley mouth and teeth and then back up the other side of her nose, round the eye and out into the other eyebrow.

I have painted golden eye shadow above green, and given her black eye liner too. Her eyes are brown. I used white acrylic paint for her eyes and teeth and added white highlights to her lips and eyes. A light blush was added to her cheeks.

I decided she needed a chin and so added it later on...when I was writing this book and decided she looks peculiar without one... look at the photo on the left below!

I had fun playing with my button stash and laid all the buttons out in the order I wanted to use them, playing around with sizes. I transferred the buttons to a tray in the same order and then marked the centre... which is very slightly off-centre... and started to sew the buttons on with doubled black thread. The big sequins are sewn on with a tiny seed bead to hold them in place.

Ginger

Meet Ginger with her zany hair style and quirky smile. She was sewn from the back after I had lightly drawn her features on in pencil first and she is one of my earlier faces. It is important to make sure the tension is slightly tighter than normal if the back of your work will be showing.

I find it a good idea to stitch the outline of the eyes from the back then add the pupils, irises and lashes from the front. Her eyebrows were made with three lines of stitch.

Ginger has lovely green eyes and blue eye shadow with rich pink lipstick. I added whites to her eyes last of all then the highlights to her lips.

Her dungarees are made from a pair of old jeans. Her skin looks a bit blotchy as she was made from a piece of hand dyed material... I think she is about to get stuck into sorting out a plumbing job!

Mirabelle

Mirabelle has been out in the sun! I chose a rich tan colour for her skin and then used a heat erasable pen to draw her features directly onto her face, but remember that the lines may re-appear in a very cold room! Use your favourite marking pen or a pencil.

I free machine stitched the left side in one go, starting from her single line eyebrow and then down into her eye, giving her plenty of eyelashes on the way. I gave her a quirky lop-sided nose to match her wonky eyes and then added heart shaped lips and a lovely swirl on one cheek and her chin. I outlined her jaw later.

I very carefully added blusher using a dry brush which I had dabbed most of the paint off first, and painted bright pink lips, deep blue eyes and lilac eye shadow.

Mirabelle's lime green dress was hand dyed and a rose appliquéd on by stitching the leaves first before the flower.

Clarissa

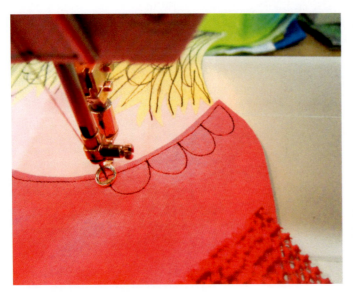

Clarissa was another face stitched from the back. I used pencil to trace her features onto the pelmet Vilene and then sewed her eyes first. You will see one is sewn with the eyebrow and nose and the other stands alone. I lifted the needle and presser foot and drew the flower on her cheek but have not cut the thread on the back to make it more secure.

One eyebrow connects the eye, nose and her mouth, which is slightly open. Her long flowing pale yellow hair was from my hand dyed stash, free machined at speed with black thread.

The flower on her cheek was painted with acrylic paint and the other cheek was dry brushed with a hint of colour.

Clarissa's dress was free machined around the neckline as you can see from the two photos above and then hand embroidered using three strands of cotton. I had to use pliers to pull the needle through the work when I was sewing the blue lazy daisy stitches!

This is a perfect opportunity to dig out all of those beads and sequins you may have bought over the years, as I have done, to add sparkle to her top.

Clementine

As I have said before, you can either machine from the front or the back of the work. Here, Clementine's features were drawn onto the back of the pelmet Vilene with a pencil and stitched from the back.

You will see that I have not followed the lines... simply used them as a bit of a guide. I find this is the easiest way to work. I didn't bother giving her an eyebrow on the side her hair covers part of her eye!

Her nose and the eyebrow on her left have just one line of stitch. I have given her blue eyes, gold eye shadow and pink lips.

Her plaited hair is made using hand dyed fabric and I stitched over and over the same lines to really emphasise the plaited look. It is worth practising on paper using a pen, to draw continuously, going over and over the lines to really make the plait stand out.

Henry

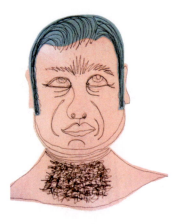

I had fun making Henry and wanted to give him a five o'clock shadow… but he seems to have rather more than that! I made him in the same way as the other faces and painted his features giving him grey shadows beneath his eyes and one side of his nose. His receding hairline was denoted by appliquéing the hair slightly higher and then adding a few strands beneath it with fast and free lines of stitch.

I used tiny hand stitches for his stubble using two strands of grey stranded cotton and seeding stitch… allowing the stitches to fall in every direction.

His eyebrows are joined up with fast and free, machine stitches. One eye, nose and mouth were connected. His cheek lines and his chin were stitched separately. I gave him a few neck folds by sewing back and forth across his neck and then into his hairy chest, described with scribble stitch.

The shirt was made using some chequered fabric which had sat in my stash for very many years. If you don't have a light box, simply tape the head onto a window and trace a shirt onto the back of the bondaweb. You will see from the picture on the right that his shoulders are higher than the original neck area shown here, below left.

I used top stitching on the collar and shirt front to make it look a bit more authentic. I shall probably add buttons to his shirt (from my huge stash!) but for now, he will do.

Helen

Helen was drawn on the back of the pelmet Vilene with pencil and then stitched from the back. If you work from the back, remember to increase the top tension slightly to pull the bobbin thread up and give a neat stitch on the back. The picture on the left was taken after hair was added! I gave her lovely bright yellow hair from my hand dyed stash and then free machine stitched over it at speed.

I painted her eyes lilac and gave her turquoise eye shadow and bright red lipstick. White was added to her eyes and I used a dry sponge to add a hint of colour to her cheeks. Picture on right.

Her dress was made with hand dyed old cotton sheeting with a golden inlay and then a machine embroidery stitch to decorate. I really must use those patterns more often!

Elaine

I have included this face as it was my first experiment with couching wool on my Sweet Sixteen and it was really fun to do. I stitched her features from the right side and then added her gingham dress. I used a double knitting yarn interlaced with pink lurex for the couching.

The couching foot has a hole in it and is a free motion foot. Make sure that the feed dogs are either down or covered when using a domestic machine. I used matching thread to sew her hair and the pink flowers and necklace. As I was stitching her long locks of hair, I just went where the needle took me... but you could draw the hair first as a guide if you prefer.

For her necklace, I started at one side and went round and round in a decreasing circle... then to the next bead, starting with a larger circle and decreasing once again. Repeat.

I started at the top left side of her dress to add the flowers, and sewed down and then into the five petal shapes, then swirled onto the next flower. Once I had finished, I threaded up my machine with black thread and free machined swirls onto each of the flower shapes as seen below.

Hilary

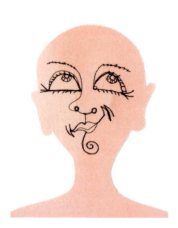   

These pictures show how Hilary was put together although I don't have a picture of her hair before it was stitched.

I free machine stitched the left side of her features in one go, starting from her eyebrow, then working down into the eye, her nose and mouth and finally her chin. I outlined her jaw later...see picture on the right.

I painted her eyes blue, added pale purple eye shadow and red lips and then painted the whites to her eyes and highlights to her lips.

She is wearing a dress with a black frill and you will see that the frill was added first, the dress ironed in place, and then the frill pulled down over the top and glued for speed! A row of top stitching would be perfect.

The purple fabric was hand dyed and then Thermofax screen printed.

Fun Face Masks!

Since I started writing this book, Covid 19 has hit the world. It is now mid May and we are well into lockdown with a very uncertain future ahead. I think that mask wearing will become the new normal… indeed, I have a wardrobe of them already so I can team up my masks with different outfits!

I hate not seeing the smiling faces we are so used to and thought a mask with a face… be it human, cat or otherwise is a good way round the problem and also they will go with anything.

I use lots of tomato puree tubes in my work and you can stitch through them easily. They do not rust and a strip just ½" wide allows the mask to conform to the bridge of your nose really well. It just means plenty of spaghetti bolognaise and chilli con carne are on the menu regularly! You can get nine or ten strips out of each tube if you are careful.

On the following pages there are full instructions for making pleated masks. The important thing to remember as you make for family and friends is the elastic length will vary accordingly. I make all my masks the same size and use 5.5" elastic for my own masks. The elastic length will vary depending for whom you are making. Size chart is on page 47.

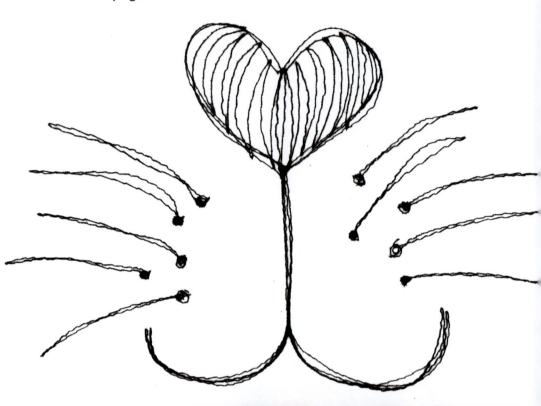

When you trace this cat face, you might prefer to shorten or lengthen the nose to mouth line to suit your own face!

I used acrylic paint for his nose but fabric paint or Inktense will also be perfect. Remember to set the colour with a hot iron.

Simply use a fine black permanent pen, if you prefer not to sew the mask. Adding the extra holes in the fabric may compromise the effectiveness of the mask… you could add a third layer of fabric for extra protection.

Using tomato puree tubes

Take great care here… when the tube is empty, use scissors to cut the top and bottom off the tube. Cut close to one side and then prise it open with a blunt knife, and wash under running water. Take care… it is very sharp! Use a boning tool or old wooden ruler to flatten out the metal. Cut into 1/2" strips with a rotary cutter if you have one and round off the four corners with small scissors or a corner rounding punch, to stop the metal poking through the fabric.

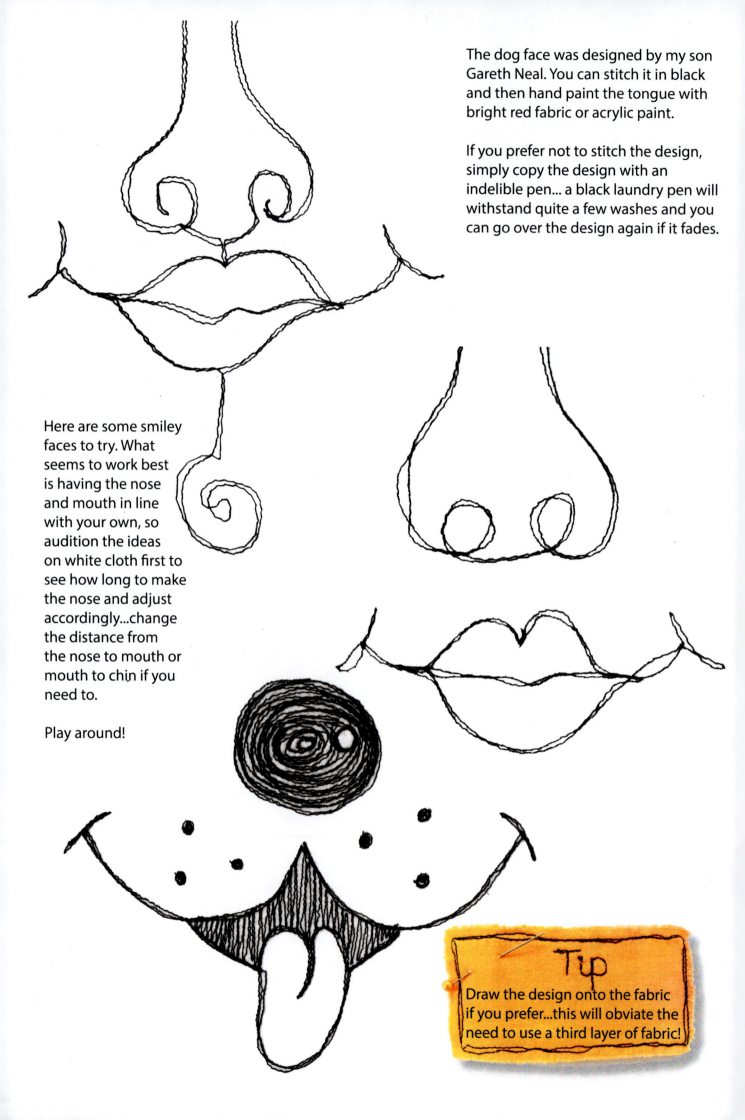

The dog face was designed by my son Gareth Neal. You can stitch it in black and then hand paint the tongue with bright red fabric or acrylic paint.

If you prefer not to stitch the design, simply copy the design with an indelible pen... a black laundry pen will withstand quite a few washes and you can go over the design again if it fades.

Here are some smiley faces to try. What seems to work best is having the nose and mouth in line with your own, so audition the ideas on white cloth first to see how long to make the nose and adjust accordingly...change the distance from the nose to mouth or mouth to chin if you need to.

Play around!

Tip
Draw the design onto the fabric if you prefer...this will obviate the need to use a third layer of fabric!

A simple, pleated, two layer mask with stiffened nose bridge

First of all you will need two pieces of white cotton... 9" wide x 6.5" deep. Position one piece over the pattern, about 1" from the top of the nose, and trace it using your choice of fabric marker. Put the fabric into a hoop and pull tight! Using black thread and the instructions given on page 14, free machine the design. Cut the threads.

Iron the fabric flat and then paint the nose using your choice of permanent paint. I use acrylic paint in crinacridone magenta. A really pretty pink colour. Allow to dry and then iron to set the colour.

Sew the golden tomato puree metal (page 40) onto the top edge of the lining fabric...allow a little more than 1/4" from the top. Sew close to the edge and secure the stitches.

Now lay the face, right side down onto the right side of the lining... the side that does not have the metal showing. The metal will not be against the skin... it will be on the inside...remember it is the top! Using white thread and sewing 1/4" from the edge, start sewing the two layers together 2" from the end, along the BOTTOM edge . *Lift the presser foot 1/4" from the end, turn the fabric and insert the elastic, lining the end of it up with the edge. Sew backwards and forwards over it at least twice.

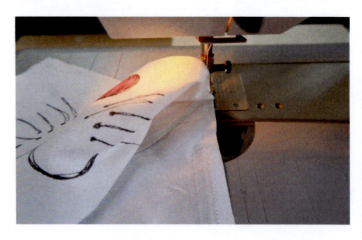

Continue to sew up the side seam... to about 1" from the end... put your hand under the fabric to find the other end of the elastic and then lift the presser foot up so you can line the elastic up, 1/4" from the top edge and sew it securely as before. *

Turn and sew across the top edge of the mask and then repeat from * to *.

Turn and sew across the bottom edge for 2" leaving a gap for turning through. Cut threads and remove from the machine.

Snip the corners off avoiding stitching and elastic! This will make the corners neater when turned through.

Turn the mask through the opening in the bottom and then press it flat, making sure the turnings match too.

Pleat the sides of the mask with three folds, down from the top, lining up both sides to make them equal. Aim for the mask to measure 2.5" deep both sides as this gives a nice snug fit on your face.

Now sew close to the edge all the way around making sure that you trap the lining opening as you go. Secure the stitching very well and then cut the threads and remove from the machine.

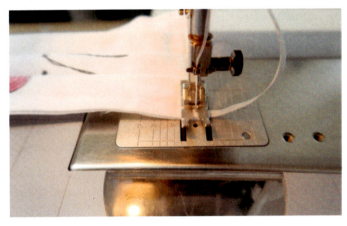

The mask is now ready to wear. Make plenty so you can wash them frequently and have different masks for all occasions! Machine washing at 60 degrees is recommended to kill viruses. Remember they are not surgical quality masks and not designed for use in a professional setting. Stay safe!

They will also be perfect for intrepid travellers to help reduce the impact of pollution travelling in a tuk-tuk in a big city or a jeep on a dusty safari ride!

Sizing guide for elastic for use with mask made from 9" wide fabric and 1/4" seams

To make sure you use the correct length of elastic, measure from your outer ear... across your nose and to the outer edge of the opposite ear. Choose a size just a little smaller so the masks fits snugly but not too tight. For hearing aid wearers, it is better to use two lengths of elastic to go around the back of the head avoiding the ears.

As a ROUGH guide, when the mask is folded in half and measured from the folded edges of the elastic...

5.5" elastic measures 13.25" (13.5cm)

6" elastic measures 13.75" (15cm)

6.5" elastic measures 14.25" (16.25cm)

7" elastic measures 14.75" (17.5cm)

7.5" elastic measures 15.25" (19cm)

I found that different widths and makes of elastic alter the fit slightly...4mm elastic works well.

You might want to make the whole mask bigger... wider and deeper if you go above this size in order to keep the proportions looking right. Experiment!

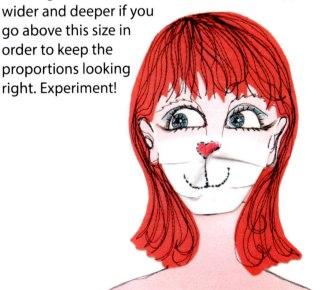

Gallery

This is the fairy, described on page 4, who looks as if she has been punched in the face and prompted me to find a better way to make faces for my quilts.

Her face was stitched last after I had enjoyed sewing her long flowing hair… it meant her face was puckered. The face should have been sewn first, but I did not have the confidence to do that.

The quilt was made way back in 2009 and is called 'Cupcake Fairy'. The original quilt measures 92 cm x 103 cm.

This is the result of my frustration… a quilt called 'Don't Forget to Drop the Dogs'. The stitcher's face, body and arms were made in the way I have described in this book.

I'm not keen on quilted skin and much prefer the smooth look. You can use the ideas in this book and work straight onto a quilt, without the use of pelmet Vilene and add quilting if you want as I did in the quilt opposite on page 47.

Susan Goodman • Sandy Hammer

ACTION BOOKS

EXPERIMENTS

Published by
New Look Books
PO Box 864
Oxford
OX2 9YD

© New Look Books Ltd 1997

All rights reserved. No part of this publication may be reproduced, stored in a retrieval system, or transmitted, in any form or by any means, electronic, mechanical, photocopying, recording or otherwise, without the written permission of the publishers.

ISBN 1-901308-06-5
British Library Cataloguing in Publication Data.
A catalogue record for this book is available from the British Library.

Printed and bound in Great Britain.

WARNING Fire is dangerous. You must do these experiments with an adult.

Fire!

In a fire, gases combine with the oxygen in the air, producing mainly heat, some light, and tiny black particles of carbon, known as 'soot'.

Experiment box

You need • candle • plasticine • bowl of water • food colour • large glass jar • matches • an adult •

1. Light a match and melt a little wax at the base of the candle. Drip the wax into the bowl and place the candle on the wax so that it is fixed there.
2. Put the jar upside down over the candle, and fix three blobs of plasticine on the bottom of the bowl so that the rim of the jar rests on them. The jar should be about 1cm above the bottom of the bowl.
3. Remove the jar. Pour water into the bowl so that it is about 1½cm deep. Add food colour to make it easier to see the water.
4. Light the candle and leave it burning for 2 minutes.
5. Cover the candle with the jar, and watch carefully.

* The candle burns for a short time and then goes out as the oxygen in the jar is used up.
* Water rises up inside the jar, taking the place of the oxygen.

To have a fire you need three things: oxygen, heat and fuel. For the fuel to burn it must be in the form of a gas; it is the heat which makes the fuel turn into a gas. Let's think about a candle. At the beginning the match provides the heat which melts some wax. This liquid wax soaks into the wick. The match heats the liquid wax. It boils. A gas is given off and the heat of the match sets fire to it. The candle can now burn without the match. The flame melts more wax, which boils on the wick, producing a gas which burns.

Under pressure

We are surrounded by a mixture of gases which we call air. Obviously air doesn't weigh very much - a bucketful weighs about the same as two pages of this book. But there is a lot of air above, pressing down on us all the time. Air pressure at sea-level is about the same as 1 kilogram pressing on every square centimetre. We don't get squashed because we have air inside us pushing out at the same pressure.

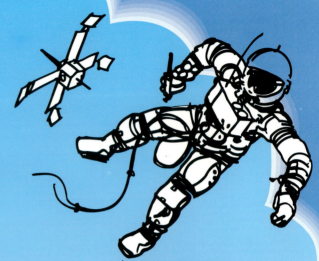

In space, men wear special pressurised suits so that the pressure inside and outside their bodies is the same as on earth.

Experiment box

You need • balloon •

1. Blow up a balloon using a pump or your lungs. Don't knot the end, pinch it closed with your fingers.
2. Let go.
3. Watch what happens and also listen carefully.

*The balloon shrinks, forcing air out, and this propels the balloon forward.

*Did you hear the high pitch sound at the end? Did you notice how hard it is to start blowing up a balloon? When a balloon is shrinking, the last little bit closes down very quickly, this pushes air out even faster and makes the sound rise sharply in pitch.

This experiment shows the way jet engines push a plane forward. They suck in air and push it out behind the plane at high speed. Rocket propulsion also depends on the force of expanding gases.

Explosive forces

Firework rockets and the huge rockets which carry satellites into space are both propelled in the same way. The fuel in the rocket burns and produces an enormous amount of gas. The gas expands and pushes down, forcing the rocket up. The cork experiment, below, demonstrates the same principle.

WARNING
Do this in the garden. Keep the cork pointing away from everyone all the time.

You need • 1 litre bottle • tightly fitting cork • vinegar • bicarbonate of soda • tissue paper • sticky tape • an adult •

1. Put about 5cms depth of vinegar in the bottle. Use a tissue to wipe the top of the bottle dry inside and out.
2. Lay a clean tissue on a flat surface. Put about two or three teaspoons of bicarbonate of soda in a line along the centre of the tissue. Roll up the tissue and turn in one end, and seal with a small strip of sticky tape. It should end up looking rather like a fat cigarette.
3. Hold the open end of the tissue package and slip it into the neck of the bottle, keeping hold of a piece of the tissue.
4. Moisten the cork with spit to help slide it into the bottle.
5. Push the cork firmly into the bottle, making sure a piece of the tissue is trapped so that the package doesn't drop into the vinegar.

POINT THE CORK AWAY FROM EVERYONE, INCLUDING YOURSELF

6. Shake the bottle so that the package is soaked in vinegar.

*When the bicarbonate of soda comes into contact with vinegar, the gas carbon dioxide is produced. The pressure builds up and ....BANG!

Most explosives work by producing a large amount of gases under pressure in some sort of container. The explosion occurs when the container can no longer withstand the build-up of pressure and breaks. This results in sudden expansion of the gases with tremendous force, sometimes enough to blow up a building. And of course there is an explosive sound.

On the surface

Look at dewdrops on a spider's web and you can see that they are tiny spheres. The reason they are round is because the molecules of water attract (pull) all the other water molecules around them. At the surface of the drop, all the molecules are pulled into the drop and the surface becomes a sphere. This pulling force is called surface tension.

Experiment box

You need • a glass • water • a cork •

1. Half fill the glass with water, look from the side at the shape of the water surface.
2. Put the cork gently on the centre of the surface. Watch the cork.
3. Fill the glass with water until it is almost spilling over. Now, what is the shape of the surface?
4. Put the cork gently on the centre of the surface? Watch the cork.

*In the half-full glass, the surface is curved downwards. The cork is pulled to the side.
*In the very full glass, the surface curves upwards. The cork sits at the high point.

Ducks float on water and stay dry, because their feathers are coated with an oily substance which repels (pushes away) water molecules.

The surface tension of the water is strong enough to support a small creature like a pond skater.

Where the action is

Experiment box

You need • paperclip • glass of water • washing-up liquid •

1. Bend up the inner piece of the paperclip so that you have something to hold onto.
2. Gently lower the flat part of the paperclip onto the surface of the water and then let go of the clip.
3. Look how it rests on the water surface.
4. Dribble a little washing-up liquid down the inside of the glass.

*The surface of the water looks as if it has a 'skin' stretched across it. This is the surface tension effect.

*As soon as the washing-up liquid touches the surface of the water, the paperclip sinks. The liquid detergent breaks the surface tension of the water.

Experiment box

You need • a soup bowl filled with milk • a soup bowl filled with water • food colour • black pepper • washing-up liquid •

1. Carefully put a few drops of food colour on the surface of the milk. Notice that they float.
2. Sprinkle black pepper on the water surface.
3. Put a little washing-up liquid on the inside edge of each of the two bowls.

*Where the detergent touches the surface of the liquid the tension is broken.

*The pepper and food colour molecules are instantly pulled to the stronger surface tension; this is on the side of the bowl opposite the point where the detergent touched the liquid surface.

Muscle bound

Almost half the weight of your body is muscle. To keep your muscles strong you need a healthy diet and exercise. Proteins build up muscle, and sugars provide energy.

Experiment box

You need • stairs • ruler • chocolate bar • to know your weight in kilograms • calculator •

1. Measure the height of a step in cms.
2. Look at the chocolate bar wrapper and find out the amount of energy in the bar. It is measured in kilojoules (kJ). For a small bar it will be about 600kJ, that's 600,000 joules.

*Energy you need to climb one step equals your weight multiplied by the height of the step, divided by 10, eg.(30kg x 20cm) ÷ 10 = 60 joules.

*Work out how many steps you have to climb to use up the energy in your chocolate bar. In our example it is:
600 000 ÷ 60 = 10 000 steps!

You use over 200 different muscles when you walk. The most powerful muscle seems to be the calf muscle. Sit a heavy person on your knees. You can raise your knees, keeping your toes on the floor, without much difficulty.

Experiment box

You need • a watch which shows seconds •

1. Put two fingertips of one hand on the inside of the wrist of the other hand, just in line with the thumb.
2. Sit quietly and count the number of throbs in a minute.

*You are measuring your heart rate. The heart pumps faster when you run and your muscles then need extra oxygen.

Good sense

We get information about the world around us from our senses. We learn to trust our sense of touch, sight, smell. But it is very easy to trick your senses - try the experiments on this page!

Experiment box

You need • a friend • blindfold • potato • apple • onion • knife •

1. Cut up the potato, apple and onion into small pieces.
2. Blindfold a friend and pinch their nose closed! Give them a piece of apple and then a piece of potato! Ask if they can taste the difference.
3. Stop pinching the nose, but keep the blindfold on. Give them a piece of apple to eat, but hold a piece of onion under their nose. What do they think they are eating?

*To taste food properly you must not only sample it in your mouth with your tongue but also smell it.

Experiment box

You need • only yourself •

1. Look at an object in the room.
2. With your eyes closed, turn around 3 times.
3. Keeping your eyes closed, point to where you think the object is.
4. Open your eyes.

*You are not pointing at the object!
*The brain uses information from our eyes and ears to determine our position. Inside our ears are tubes of liquid which send messages to the brain. When we spin round with our eyes closed, the messages from the swirling liquid in our ears confuse our brain.

Highly strung

Experiment box

You need • a plastic ruler • a wooden ruler •

1. Hold the ruler firmly on the edge of a table so that about 5cm sticks over the edge.
2. Twang the ruler. Listen to the sound and watch how fast the ruler vibrates.
3. Push the ruler further over the edge of the table and repeat instructions 1 and 2.
4. Continue until most of the ruler sticks out over the table edge.

*The vibrating ruler produces a sound. The slower the vibrations, the deeper the sound.

*Your plastic ruler might be so bendy (flexible) that, when it is projecting a long way over the edge of the table, it vibrates very slowly, and you hear nothing.

Anything you can hear is a sound. Sounds are made when something makes air move backwards and forwards (vibrate) quite fast.

Experiment box

You need • a mixture of elastic bands (thick, thin, long, short) • an empty plastic box (or tin) with lid •

1. Stretch an elastic band between two fingers and twang it.
2. Stretch it further and twang again. Listen and watch the band.
3. Try the same with other elastic bands.
4. Put the bands over the plastic box with the lid on and twang them. Repeat with the lid off.

*The air in the box vibrates and the twanging of the elastic band is louder.

*Look at violins, cellos, guitars. They all basically have strings stretched across boxes.

Banging about

Native Americans are sometimes shown in films with an ear pressed to the ground listening for the distant rumble of horse hoofs. You can try this but you are more likely to hear the rumble of lorries!

Sound does not only travel through air. Vibrations can travel through many substances, including water, glass, wood, and concrete. Sound travels especially easily through water, and the noise that whales make can be heard through hundreds of kilometres of ocean.

Experiment box

You need • a friend • wooden table •

1. Ask your friend to sit at the opposite end of the table and gently scratch the surface.
2. Listen to the sound and then press your ear onto the surface of the table.

*The sound is much louder when you listen to it travelling through wood rather than through air.

You need • a large round empty tin or bowl • thin plastic bag •

1. Cut the plastic bag open and make sure it is large enough to cover the tin.
2. Make a drum by stretching the plastic over the top of the tin and holding it in place with an elastic band stretched round the tin.
3. Sprinkle a teaspoon of sugar over the plastic.
4. Hold the metal tray close to your drum and bang it slowly with the wooden spoon.

*The sugar bounces up and down.
*Banging the metal tray makes the air around it vibrate. These vibrations (sound waves) move through the air and hit the stretched plastic, making it vibrate too. The slight movement in the plastic makes the sugar jump up.
*When sound waves from the metal tray reach your ears, you hear the bang.

Experiment box

Hot air

When air gets hot it takes up more space (expands) and becomes lighter; so it floats upward. Hot-air balloons have a burner in the basket to heat up the air in the balloon and make it rise higher.

Experiment box

You need • bottle • balloon • bowl of cold water •

1. Fill the bottle with hot water from the tap.
2. Cut most of the neck off a balloon.
3. Pour hot water out of the bottle.
4. Pull the balloon neck down over the top of the bottle.
5. Stand the bottle in a bowl of cold water and watch what happens. You could also pour cold water over the upper part of the bottle which is not in the cold water. This will cool the air in the bottle even more.

*The hot water heats the bottle and this makes the air inside the bottle hot.
*As the air is cooled and 'shrinks' ('contract' is the proper word), the balloon is sucked into the bottle.
*Take the bottle out of the cold water and stand it in a warm room. Watch what happens as the cold air in the bottle begins to expand.

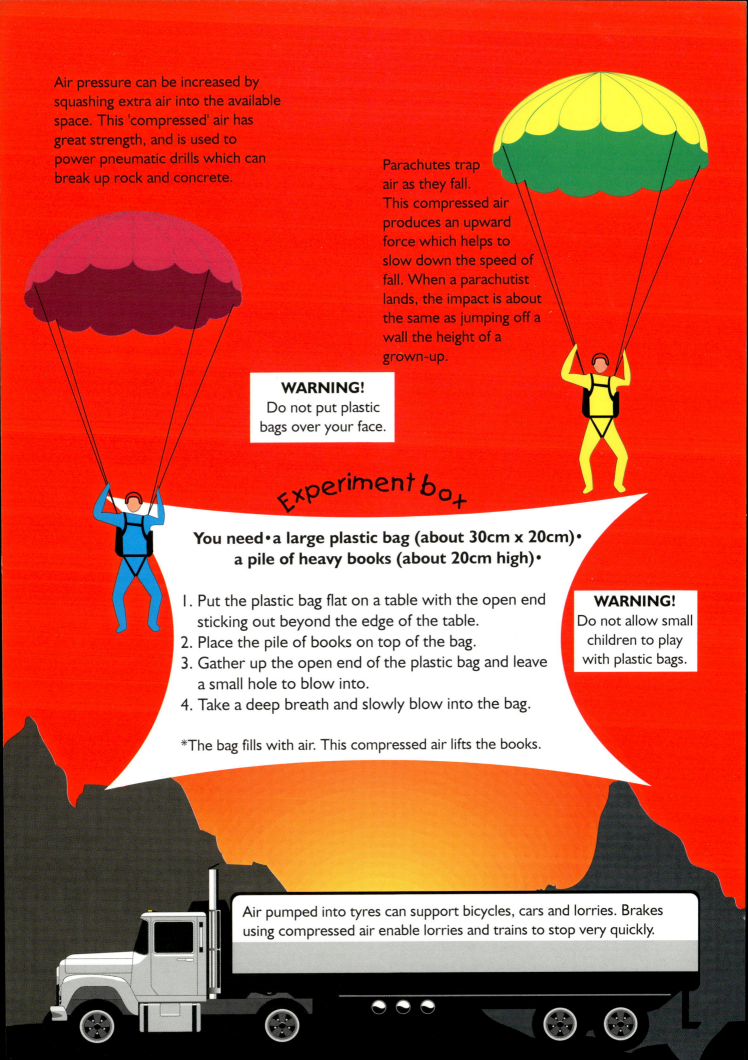

In the kitchen

In the kitchen everyone can be a scientist. Watch carefully and keep asking questions. Why does baking a cake turn it from a sloppy liquid to a firm sponge? What happens when you boil a potato, or fry an egg? The answers aren't always simple. It might be years before you fully understand. But do keep asking science questions and one day you might be a scientist.

WARNING Make sure an adult helps you with all these kitchen experiments.

Experiment box

You need • ½ cup sugar • ½ cup water • saucepan • cooker • an adult •

1. Mix sugar and water in the saucepan to make a sugar solution.
2. Carefully heat up the sugar solution and let it cook until it changes to dark brown.
3. Leave to cool. Add water to dissolve some of the brown caramel. Taste.

*Heating has caused a chemical change and destroyed the sugar. All that is left is carbon - the same as you get on burnt toast.

Experiment box

You need • red cabbage • water • saucepan • cooker • knife • sieve • glass jar with lid • 4 small glasses • lemon juice • vinegar • bicarbonate of soda • general household cleaner • an adult •

1. Cut the red cabbage into pieces and put into a saucepan of water. Bring to the boil and leave to cool.
2. Pour through a sieve and keep the deep purple liquid in a jar with a lid.
3. Dissolve a few spoonfuls of bicarbonate of soda in a little water in a glass. Put lemon juice, vinegar and household cleaner in each of the other glasses.
4. Pour some of the cabbage water into each glass.

*The cabbage water is called an 'indicator'. It changes colour and shows ('indicates') what sort of liquid you have. Is it an acid, like lemon juice? Or an alkali, like bicarbonate of soda?

*Try some other liquids, e.g. fruit juices, liquids from tinned food, cooking water from vegetables.

What's cooking?

WARNING Always do these experiments with an adult. They can be dangerous.

Experiment box

You need • popping corn • saucepan with lid • oil • cooker • an adult •

1. Put a little oil at the bottom of a saucepan and heat up gently.
2. When the oil is hot put a spoonful of popping corn in the saucepan and put the lid on the saucepan.
3. Turn the heat off when the popping sound stops.

*Popping corn are the seeds (or 'kernels') of the maize plant. They look dry and dead. But all seeds contain a tiny amount of water that keeps the cells alive until they are in the right conditions to grow.

*When you heat the popcorn, the water inside boils. The steam pushes with enormous pressure on the tough outer seed-coat. It bursts and the softer inside of the seed puffs up.

Experiment box

You need • dried yeast • sugar • glucose • cornflour • salt • several glasses • teaspoons • hand-hot water • cardboard covers for glasses • an adult •

1. Dissolve two teaspoons of each of the following substances in four separate glasses of hand-hot water: sugar, glucose, cornflour, salt.
2. Add a teaspoon of dried yeast to each glass and stir.
3. Cover the glasses with cardboard covers to keep the contents of the glass warm. (You could stand them in a bowl of hand-hot water).

*Where possible the yeast will produce sugars it can feed on. It will also produce bubbles of the gas carbon dioxide.

*By watching the yeast growing in the glasses you will be able to decide which foods yeast feeds on. Also note which food makes yeast grow most quickly. Try some other foods.

Yeasts are very important in baking, wine-making and brewing beer.

They are tiny one-celled plants which, like mushrooms, do not have chlorophyll (the green substance which enables most plants to make their own food from sunlight, water and carbon dioxide).

Yeasts have special chemicals, called 'enzymes', to change starches into the sugars it feeds on.

Tree tops

When a tree has been cut down you can see a series of rings across the tree trunk. A new ring is produced each year. Count the rings and you can find, very accurately, the age of the tree. You can also tell which years had warm, wet, growing weather. In those years the rings will be thicker, showing extra growth. In years of drought the rings will be very narrow.

Experiment box

You need • a friend • a large tree •

1. Ask your friend to stand by a tree.
2. Hold your thumb up at arm's length.
3. Close one eye and walk backwards, carefully. Look all the time at your thumb and stop when it appears the same size as your friend.
4. Now move your thumb up slowly, and count how many times your thumb can fit into the height of the tree. Remember this number.
5. Multiply this number by the height of your friend and you have the height of the tree.

Experiment box

You need • mature tree • tape measure •

1. Measure round the tree trunk.

* Most tree trunks increase by about 2.5cm a year.
* Divide your tree measurement by 2.5 to get the approximate age of the tree.

Suprisingly, the roots of a tree do not go very far into the ground. A tree 50m tall (that is about five times the height of a house) has roots that only go 2.5m into the ground (about double your height). But they can spread out about the same distance as the height of the tree. The roots of a 50m tree will cover the same area as a football pitch.

Rising sap

Experiment box

You need • tree • plastic bag • string • a hot sunny day •

1. Put a plastic bag over a small tree-branch in full sun.
2. Tie the open end of the bag around the branch with string, so that the leaves are sealed in the bag.

*After a few hours, water droplets collect in the bag. The water comes out of the tree through tiny holes in the leaves.

Just below the surface of the bark of a tree is a living layer called 'sapwood'. Up through this layer, water and minerals pass from the tree roots in the earth to the leaves. In hot weather a mature birch tree can take up more than 50 big buckets of water. This water passes out of small holes in the leaves.

Experiment box

You need • white carnation • two different food colours • two yogurt pots filled with water •

1. Add a few drops of food colour to one yogurt pot and a few drops of the second colour to the other yogurt pot.
2. Make a split in the carnation stem, from the bottom, about 10cms in length.
3. Put one half of the stem in one pot, the other half in the other pot.
4. Leave in a warm room for a few hours.

*One half of the carnation will change into one of the colours, the other half into the other colour.
*This shows that pathways up the stem lead to particular parts of the plant.

Party tricks

Coin conundrum

You need • a glass • coin • playing card •

1. Place the card on top of the glass.
2. Place the coin on the centre of the card.
3. Flick the card off the glass.

*The card moves forward and the coin drops into the glass.
* There isn't a force making the coin fly across the table with the card.

Glass surprise

You need • a glass • water • piece of card (size of postcard) •

DO THIS TRICK OVER A BOWL IN CASE IT DOESN'T WORK!
1. Fill the glass with water until overflowing.
2. Place the card firmly on top of the glass.
3. Hold the card in place with the palm of your hand.
4. Turn the glass upside down.
5. Remove your hand!
6. Smoothly turn the glass and card up the right way, and then upside down again.

*The card stays in place because of air pressure pushing on it.

Box of tricks

You need • an empty box with lid • small heavy weight • sticky tape •

1. Tape the heavy weight in the corner of the box and put the lid on the box.
2. Place the box on the table. Slowly slide it off the table until only the corner with the weight is on the table.

*The box looks as though it is hanging in the air, but of course, the unseen weight keeps it firmly on the table.

Magic moments

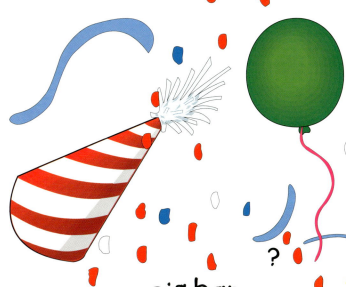

Dancing raisins

You need • drinking glass • raisins • fizzy drink •

1. Put a few raisins in the bottom of the glass.
2. Pour fizzy drink into the glass.

*Bubbles of carbon dioxide are dissolved in the fizzy drink.
*Bubbles form on the raisins, making them lighter; so they float to the surface.
*Bubbles burst at the surface of the drink, and the raisins then sink back to the bottom of the glass.

Big bang

You need • balloon • pin • transparent sticky tape •

1. Blow up the balloon and knot the neck.
2. Put a 1cm square of transparent sticky tape on the side of the balloon.
3. Stick the pin through the sticky tape on the balloon!

*The balloon does not go bang. The sticky tape stops the pinhole from tearing and so prevents air rushing out of the balloon in an explosion.

Magic bubbles

You need • bubble mixture • bubble frame •

1. Dip your finger in the bubble mixture.
2. Dip the bubble frame in the bubble mixture and gently blow a large bubble. Do not blow it off the frame.
3. Put your finger into the bubble!

*The bubble doesn't burst but instead forms a bubble round your finger.
*Of course a dry finger will burst the bubble. You could ask people watching to try it.

High fliers

Have you ever wondered how aeroplanes can fly? How do such large, heavy objects get up high into the sky? Do the simple experiments on these two pages and you'll soon understand the secret of flight.

Experiment box

You need • two balloons • string or cotton • a stick, a metre long • two stools or kitchen chairs •

1. Blow up two balloons and knot them.
2. Cut two 30cm lengths of string.
3. Tie each balloon to a piece of string.
4. Tie the other ends of the strings to a stick, so that the strings are about 40cm apart.
5. Put two chairs back to back so that they are just under a metre apart. Or use two stools. Rest the stick on them.
6. Kneel down and blow between the balloons.

*The balloons move closer together!
*Moving air has less pressure, less pushing power than still air. The air on the side of the balloons nearer the stools has more push than the air you have blown away. So, the balloons are pushed together.

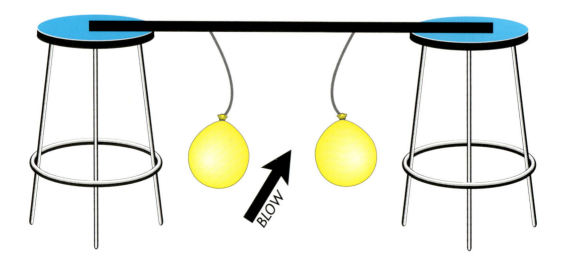

Experiment box

You need • a strip of paper (about 5cms x 20cms) •

1. Hold one end of the paper just below your lips.
2. Blow down, along the paper.

*The paper isn't blown downwards. It lifts.
*The air pressure above the paper was reduced when you blew. So the air pressure under the paper was greater than that above it. The paper therefore lifted up.

Aeroplanes are lifted into the air, because air pressure under the wings is greater than the pressure above. As an aeroplane speeds along the runway, air rushes over the wings. The top is curved to make the air move faster, and so reduce the pressure above the wings. The plane goes faster, the pressure above the wings drops, and the greater air pressure under the wing lifts the aeroplane into the sky. This upward force is greater than the pull of gravity, which is pulling the plane downwards - back to the ground!

Thought experiments

The great scientist, Albert Einstein, used thought experiments to help him develop his amazing relativity theories about space and time. He used these imaginary experiments because it wasn't actually possible at that time to do the experiments he thought up. More recently, with modern developments in science and technology, some of these experiments have become possible and when they are done the results turn out to be exactly as Einstein had predicted.

You can have fun trying to think up thought experiments and seeing if you can solve them in your brain.

Q• You have a bottle one-third filled with vinegar and one-third filled with oil. You want only vinegar on your chips and oil on your lettuce. How can you get each separately from this bottle?

A• Remember, oil floats on vinegar. You can pour oil from the top of the bottle. Turn the bottle upside down and now the vinegar is next to the lid.

Q• When we breathe in air, we use some of the oxygen and breathe out extra carbon dioxide. With so many millions of people breathing all the time, why don't we run out of oxygen?

A• All green plants take in carbon dioxide and give out the oxygen essential for us to live.

Keep thinking?

Q • What's wrong with the following statements?
1. When an astronaut first landed on the moon, he stuck a pole with a flag in the ground and watched it flutter in the breeze.
2. He saw a meteor glowing as it raced towards the moon's surface.
3. He was startled after he knocked a boulder - it rolled, crashing noisily into a crater.

A • 1. There's no air on the moon so there is no wind to blow a flag.
2. Meteors only burn and glow as they fall through air and are subject to air resistance.
3. There is no sound without air.

Q • Imagine a hole dug right through the moon from one side to the other. What happens if you drop a ball into one end of the hole?

A • The ball will be pulled by gravity to the centre of the moon. It will go faster and faster, reaching its greatest speed at the moon's centre. It will then slow down until it reaches the other end of the hole, where it will fall back down the hole. It will go backwards and forwards for ever.

Sometimes scientists think of unusual experiments which they would like taken into space on a Space Shuttle to see what happens in zero gravity. Here are some possible ideas: What sort of web would a spider make in space? What happens to a candle flame in zero gravity? Can you think of an interesting experiment to do in space? Please write to us, at New Look Books-we'd love to hear about it. Our address is near the beginning of this book.

Happy thinking!

Science words

Air is a mixture of gases: 78% nitrogen, 21% oxygen, 1% other gases, including carbon dioxide.

Air pressure is produced by the air that is all around us. At sea level it is about 1kg pressing on one square centimetre, but as you go up mountains, it gets less. At heights above 300m you can begin to feel breathless and short of oxygen.

Atmosphere is the layer of air wrapped around the Earth.

Atoms are the smallest bits of an **element**.

Condensation is the tiny drops of water you see on cold things when the air has a lot of water vapour in it.

Contract means to shrink or get smaller, (opposite: **expand**).

Elements are only made of one type of **atom**. There are about 107 in nature. They include: oxygen, carbon, iron, hydrogen, aluminium. Everything in the whole universe is made up of different combinations of these 107 elements.

Expand means to get bigger. This often happens because something has got hotter. Even buildings expand a little. The Empire State Building in New York is about 15cm taller on a hot day than on a cold day.

Filtering is the separation of solid particles from a liquid. This is done by passing the mixture through a filter, something with small holes which traps the particles.

Friction is a force which tends to stop things sliding over each other.

Fuel is a substance used for producing heat.

Gravity is the force which keeps us on the Earth and stops us, and other objects, flying off into space. It is a pulling force which acts between all objects and is greater the larger the object.

Molecules are the smallest particles of a particular substace. They are made up of **atoms**.

Surface tension exists at the surface of all liquids, and is due to the way the liquid molecules pull at each other. It causes a surface to behave as if it has an elastic skin.

Water vapour is made of water droplets, so tiny that you can't see them. When the vapour condenses onto something cold, the water droplets can be seen. (See **Condensation**).